# A Murmuration of Words

*poems by*

# Martha Royster

*Finishing Line Press*
Georgetown, Kentucky

# A Murmuration of Words

**Between a
Charm of Hummingbirds
and a
Labor of Moles**

## ACKNOWLEDGMENTS

Thank you to my family who make the garden possible. Thank you to
Jacob for the right support at just the right moment. Thank you to Kelly for
nudging the dream. Thank you to my father for the gift of many beautiful
notebooks over the years and the admonishment to "just write." Thank you
to Dan, for everything. Thank you to Finishing Line Press for helping me
find the courage to be brave.

Publisher: Leah Huete de Maines
Editor: Christen Kincaid
Cover Art: Martha Royster
Author Photo: Martha Royster
Cover Design: Elizabeth Maines McCleavy


Order online: www.finishinglinepress.com
also available on amazon.com

Author inquiries and mail orders:
Finishing Line Press
PO Box 1626
Georgetown, Kentucky 40324
USA

# Contents

## WINTER'S PROMISE

Tender shoots push their way through
cold soil and autumn leaves
seeking the sun's warmth

Lean fish, hungry from a long winter's rest
surface to curiously explore the water's edge

Tiny bees crawl from the warm safety their mother built for them
where they have waited long months for this day

Weary travelers making the long flight north
grateful for a place to rest
share their songs

Cherry blossoms falling gently
a memory of January snow

Winter's quiet patience fades
Spring returns

## THE MIST

As twilight squeezes light from the pale winter sky
tendrils of mist begin to rise
from the cold ground
where they have been held captive all day
barely trapped by the sun's weak winter warmth
rising slowly to fill the space between
damp earth and grey sky
The wisps swirl like lost souls
call down the darkness to surround them, fill them
become opaque shadows in the cold winter night
a boon for hungry predators
rising at day's end to begin their work

## SCENT OF DEATH

The Scent of Death lingers
cold grey ashes
long after the fire is gone

It is carried by the wind
through the air to the red dog
who lifts her nose to catch the familiar scent

It swirls in pools and eddies
around fading roses
and browning hollyhocks

It rises high into the slate sky
catches the attention
of circling vultures

It brushes gently over
the tiny still hummingbird
its iridescent red throat the color of blood against the white snow

It slowly fades
waits to be summoned
once again

## WINTER CHORES

Toes encased in warm wool socks
slip into cold boots stiff with yesterday's mud
A warm green coat is zipped snugly
the faint suggestion of lanolin in the air
hints at the origins of the grey knitted hat
from the grazing sheep who turn
sunlight into warm spotted coats

Boots crunch noisily across the frozen grass
pass through swirls of excitement hanging in the air
left behind by the warm breath of eager dogs
running circles in their warm spotted winter coats

Chickens barely discernible in the early morning dark
chat noisily to each other
over their bowls of grain in the warm barn
Their morning gift already given
warm in the straw nest
Eggs
greens and browns the colors of spring

## FOG

Valleys become white seas
trees become islands
as the cold fog seeps in to fill the spaces

The fog seems to consume me as well
I watch my warm breath transform into a swirling white mist

The forest disappears and reappears as I walk
Hidden
then revealed

## GREETING DEATH

When the days remaining
were counted on one hand
a beloved beagle prepares to greet death

She asks to go out into the crisp, winter garden
her hard-fought thin breath visible in the frosty air
She slowly
painfully
stubbornly
makes her way
through the frozen grass
to her favorite spots in the garden

Bricks warm in the summer sun now covered with a sparkling sugar
coating of ice
Shade of the huge maple now bare branches casting skeleton shadows
below
A green meadow where dogs play now hidden in the thick grey fog
The tantalizing scent of ripe apples now a memory as bare trees brace
for winter
Evergreens filled with birdsong now quiet bending to whirling wind

She fills her slowing heart with peace from her garden
Familiar warm hands gently help her settle in the soft bed
And she waits

## SURPRISED BY HOPE

A small bulb carefully planted
the site thoughtfully chosen in the soft earth beneath tall pine trees

Gentle spring rains fall
no soft green shoots appear

Warm summer sunlight filters through sheltering pine branches
fall winds spread pine needles on the ground
winter turns the earth hard and cold

Spring comes again
no soft green shoots appear

Weeds are pulled around the bulb
happy dogs run by in the summer sun chasing Frisbees
and each other
squirrels bury precious fall nuts in the soft soil
winter's quiet settles over the garden

Spring comes again
no soft green shoots appear

Noisy blue jays build a nest in the branches above
busy bees collect pollen from the sea of flowers
open in the summer sun
fall leaves pile up over the bulb

A late winter snow unexpectedly chills the warming soil
and a small, fragile looking shoot picks this time
to push its way, at last, toward the sunlight
Three characteristic leaves unfurl
the long awaited magnificent white bloom appears
when it is least expected
most needed
cherished more

## COME TO MY MEADOW

Our world is transformed

I can see it
 in the nervous eyes of the soft doe
 as she searches for a place safe from fast cars

Come to my meadow
there is tall grass to eat and
trees to shelter young

I can see it
 in the lifeless eyes of the thin snakes
 who did not survive the search for safety

Come to my meadow
there are fat mice to eat
and sun warmed rocks for shelter

I can see it
 in the resigned eyes of the dry, dust covered newt
 as he slowly walks on and on, hoping to find water

Come to my meadow
there is a gentle creek to cool your skin
and shady ferns for shelter

I can see it
 in the wary eyes of the owl
 as she mourns the loss of her nest
 cut down to make room for more of us

Come to my meadow
there is dinner waiting in the dark grass
and trees still stand tall to shelter new nests

I can see it
in the sad eyes in the mirror
as we argue, blame, and deny
our world is transformed

Come to my meadow
hope lives here

## FIRST FLIGHT

Six colorful new hens, stunning black, white, and copper feathers
learn the rules of the barnyard
wait to fill their hungry bellies
after the older hens have eaten
quickly strikes the vanguard
to snatch a mouthful

In the first hint of dawn
when night's shadow still clings to familiar shapes
six little hens wait at the door of the sturdy pen
where they shelter at night
Safe from the vigilant owl
hunting for something for the hungry bellies in her full nest

When the door swings open, five hens quickly fly out
spread their new wings to easily glide
the short distance to the ground
The sixth hen, carefully considers and then bravely follows

The first day she overshoots and hits the post
The second day, she considers longer and adjusts, missing the post,
collides with the fence
The third day, she waits a long time
toes gripping the door's edge, her bright eyes looking around her
quickly
up, down, side to side over and over
Then she leaps
soars briefly through the cool, morning air
avoiding post and fence she settles quite gracefully
on the top roosting bar
Far exceeding the skill required for a quick glide to the ground
She looks around
ruffles her feathers in satisfaction
and hops down to join her sisters

## DOGWOODS

Dogwoods planted
as saplings
form a green thicket
spring branches heavy with new leaves
reach for the sun
tall, vigorous trees never flower

Until the grove shares its peace
shelters near its bare winter stand
the final rest of a beloved companion
then delicate white flowers appear in spring

## QUIET

Before the sunrise
Before the bird song
Before the day begins
the garden is filled with quiet

Hello friend

Quiet is not
an absence of sound
a void
nothingness

Quiet is
the space before the beginning
alive with possibility
the place where dreams wait

## SAFETY OF SOLITUDE

She pushes the shopping cart with the squeaky, erratic wheel
to the dark, deserted store, its windows obscured
by graffiti covered plywood
She passes the fallen sign, reminding her to wear a mask
and wash her hands
fills her cart with canned and colorful boxes of food
and bottles of water

She has cleared herself a path in the empty street
around discarded signs with faded, angry words
avoiding glittering piles of shattered glass
past the blackened shells of burnt cars to her safe lair
in the dark basement
She stops and picks up an object reflecting the sun's relentless heat
slips it quickly into her pocket

She pushes the heavy cart faster, glancing quickly around
listening intently for danger
All that remains of a flag, tattered strips the color of blood
hangs lifeless from its tall pole in overheated, still air
She hides the precious shopping cart in the hallway
and makes many trips up and down the stairs with her provisions

She takes a water bottle and a box of cereal
garishly covered with cartoon characters she can no longer name,
climbs
past glassless window frames and empty doorless apartments
to the roof

She spends most of her days up here
in the light
only returning to the safety of the dark, unlit basement at night
Crouching in the stingy shade
tending a small, hidden roof top garden
spending her precious water to nourish thirsty plants
At first, when she looked out over the vast ruin of the city
spread out below her,

she wondered
if there were others like her, survivors of virus and violence

But now, she has learned to cherish the safety of solitude
She reaches into the pocket of her filthy jacket and pulls out
the object she picked up earlier, she fingers the still shiny silver dollar
once the all-important foundation on which their society was built
now a piece of metal bearing the image of a long dead man
Valueless
She reaches back and throws it high into the air
It turns over and over, spiraling in the bright blue sky before
landing once again amid the rubble below

## ONE YELLOW BIRD

Summer, fall and winter she waits
for the return of the goldfinches
As spring begins to push winter aside
she searches every day among the many winged visitors
Every day eagerly anticipating their arrival
Are they here yet?
Have they arrived?
Will they return?

At last, they finally appear
bursting into the garden with their bright yellow coats,
jaunty black caps, and cheerful song
The sight of the first brings joy

As more arrive every day
she forgets to be surprised
Becomes nonchalant
Desensitized
Complacent
She forgets to notice

Fields of crimson clover put on a spectacular show
undulations of dark red between green fields and blue sky
Hoping to catch our eye
Pierce our complacency
Impress
More than a cover crop planted to prepare the way
for something better
Be noticed

A plain brown bag set casually on the table
In the before, its contents unimpressive in our complacency
today eagerly anticipated
two red and white bags of flour
made precious by their scarcity

One bright yellow bird perched atop the rose bush
surrounded by buds whose opening is eagerly anticipated
His sharp black eyes demand notice
Catch my eye
Admonish against complacency
Before he quickly disappears

# TIME CAPSULE

The small, battered tube protects a time capsule of the previous spring
His mother collected pollen from last year's flowers
on which to carefully place his egg
a captured memory of spring to nourish him
safe in his nest

In summer
as the heat dome crushed the garden
scorching leaves to fall's crumbling brown in a day

In fall
as ash, remains of trees devoured by wildfires,
turned skies to winter dark
piled up on the ground
a cruel afterimage of snow

In winter
as another wave washes over carrying yet a new variant
civilizations, weary, turn on each other in anger
lines are drawn, earth scorched

His mother anticipated none of this when she collected pollen
placed the nest close to the cherry tree
she hopes will still be there for him

She captured a small sampling of time to sustain him
she would not be there
that was not her role

Weak winter sun warms the mud seal
He pushes through
finally making an opening
Like turning the wheel and opening the heavy hatch of a shelter
peering out,
is it safe?

He squeezes out
waits for the winter sun to warm him
and stretches his new wings
before he flies

## FLEDGLING

The small brown body lies broken and bloody, lifeless
Her tan and black feathers still hold the shine of new
Do her parents mourn her?
Do they still hold the illusion that she fledged
is out in the garden stretching new wings?

A young soldier's still body lies broken in a burnt orchard
The fire scarred trees wear no leaves to soften the sun's light
No fruit will grow here
In his hand he tightly cherishes cookies from home
As he died under the trees
his thoughts slowly stopped along with his young heart
Were they thoughts of home?
Coming home after school to climb an apple tree
Warm cookies taken from a pocket and enjoyed
from the highest branch
while he surveyed the world beyond the garden

A lone bird lands on one of the scorched trees
She shares no song
Nests will no longer find shelter in this orchard
among the rustling green leaves
The scent of fruit ripening in the sun
will no longer be carried by the breeze over the garden wall
There will be no fat worms in the cool grass under the trees
to feed hungry hatchlings
Bird song will not greet the dawn from this orchard

The fetor of death hangs in the still air
She spreads her wings
circles over the remains below
her bright eyes capturing the devastation
She climbs higher into the summering sky
searching for a safe place to rest on her long journey
She will not return here

# PEACE

Patches of sunlight filter through the tall trees
dappled by cool, green pine needles
as they mark circles of warmth on the grass below

Elegant and majestic, the queen of the garden
stands tall above her peers
her colorful buds and magnificent blossoms
an inspiration
her leaves make cool shade for the flowers at her feet

Aerial acrobats swoop, hum, hover, and soar
their wings a flash of green, yellow, blue, and red in the warm sunlight
as they build nests and raise young

Creek sounds, water gently moving pebbles
invites visitors
a cool drink
a cool dip
a shady rest

Energetic bees mark a path between flowers
warmed and opened by the sunlight
their gift to all of us
to ensure the garden continues

## THE GIFT

A clean sheet of paper
crisp, white, smelling new

A bright yellow pencil
its tip sharpened to a thin point

She observes
playful dogs running in the fresh mowed grass
a colorful hummingbird exploring a feast of blossoms
glimpses of the bright red head of the noisy woodpecker

The paper is blank

She listens
to woods filled with birdsong
the buzz of lumbering bumblebees heavy with pollen
hens noisily congratulating each other on this day's work

The pencil is still

The promise filled light of a new day
stretches over the awakening garden

She waits

The poem is a gift
given when it is ready
to be received
can't be rushed or hurried

She waits

Ah, here it is
given at last
The pencil scratches quickly
the words spill across the paper

The gift received

## CARRIED ON THE WIND

Trees bow, creaking and groaning
in the path of the hot, roaring, smoke-filled wind
bending close to breaking point
the ground littered with leaves and branches
jettisoned cargo following a foundering ship
their summer parched branches coated with ash
carried hundreds of miles by the relentless wind
all that remains of other trees, burned by wildfires far away
smoke, ash, and heat blown in to fill our safe haven
reminds that what touches one

Touches all

## WORKING DOG

Alert brown eyes sprinkled with blue survey the horizon
from her post in the cool shade of the cedar trees
A working dog who has chosen
to keep watch
over me

All day she is my quiet companion
every place my work in the garden takes me
she settles down patiently
to keep watch
over me

Ensuring I am
kept safe
never alone
never lonely
she keeps watch
over me

When the sun sets on the busy garden
she finally seeks her soft bed
her tired eyes reluctantly close
and I keep watch
over her

## TRACES

Dark stains on the rocks
dry slowly
Splashed by energetic early morning bathers

Blue feathers striped boldly with black
lay shimmering
Shed in the dew dampened grass

Tiny, shattered remains of a bright blue shell
crumble unnoticed
No longer enfolding a new bird

Red, yellow, purple, and pink rose petals
settle hidden
Barely discernible beneath pine needles

Traces in the still summer garden
give witness to its inhabitants

## WATER IS

Jewels sparkling in the sunlight
adorning a spider's web

A gentle rain lightly touching leaves
providing an oasis for
the garden's tiniest inhabitants

Big, noisy raindrops plopping loudly on the ground
their arrival announced by thunder and lightning
gratefully received by thirsty plants

The shadowy realm for the colorful fish
the earthbound plants above
reflected on the dark mirror surface
we look through an image of our world to glimpse theirs

A cool refreshing drink
in my frosty glass
in the silver bowl at my feet
for the thirsty gardener and
happy, panting dogs

Two hydrogen connected by oxygen
their difference what binds them together
their whole stronger than the parts

Water is the magic
that makes all things possible

## RECOVERY

Sleepy hands trade slippers for sneakers
A leash is clipped on a weary companion
Illness necessitates a change in the routine

A walk in the day's early cool
before summer heat shimmers the air
In the cool silver light of a summer morning
as the night sky slowly unfurls to robin's egg blue

Soon the air will fill with birdsong and buzzing
now there is silence

A doe and her twin fawns
their coats freckled with a constellation of spots
turn their heads and gaze at us
as they leave the nighttime safety of the pasture

Just glimpsed disappearing around a bend in the creek
the last few in a long line of ducklings

A red-tailed hawk stands on a fence post
enjoying a successful hunt
where recently a great horned owl perched
enjoying her successful hunt

I slow my steps as my companion conquers the hill
think this inconvenience
interruption of the busy, full schedule
feels like a gift
My companion turns his face to look up at me
his eyes mirror the same thought

# THE HUMMINGBIRD

Perched high in the rhododendron
safely camouflaged by the cool green leaves
her bright eyes watch the sprinkler's arc
leave wet, silvery trails on the grass

She waits as it oscillates back and forth

When the sprinkler finally stops
she quickly hops onto a branch of
the glistening red maple tree
the tiny droplets of water a gift to her

She drinks her fill
then quickly siphons up the water drops
places them to roll down her back, her breast, her wings
her stunning colors reflecting the sun's brilliance

She must work quickly as the sun's greedy light is already
stealing the precious tiny drops from the leaves

She lingers a few moments longer amid the bright red maple leaves
enjoying the warmth on her damp feathers
while the maple tree quickly returns its sparkle to the sun

## AUTUMN'S CLOAK

The quiet sky shatters open
noisy wild geese pour through
the V shaped opening
They carry fall with them
through the crack high in the sky
their powerful wings drape an autumn cloak
over the landscape far below
summer green turns to brilliant fall
except conifers' stubborn defiance
evergreen among hillsides aflame with reds, oranges, yellows
the geese disappear into a tiny black dot
the quiet sky returns
but nothing is the same

# FALL

Playful dogs ignite a contrail of color
as they run through leaves

Ruby, gold, emerald, amber and bronze shimmer
bright against the slate sky
settle softly
to pile haphazardly
in the wet, green grass

Flame colored trees cascade down
pine covered hills
the horizon engulfed in fall's spectacular colors

Crisp green apples with summer's red blush
encased in fall's frost
suspended from leafless branches

The enveloping grey fog alive
with the honking of noisy migrating wild geese
faint silhouettes that disappear
and reappear in the mist overhead

Educated at Mills College in Biochemistry and German Studies, Martha lives in the Pacific Northwest tending a small waypoint under the Pacific Flyway in a garden surrounded by birds, butterflies, and a lot of roses. While poetry is often an illusion, there is a real garden at the creative heart of these poems. The inspiration for this collection comes through a garden transitioning from a small family farm to a wildlife habitat. During this land rehabilitation project Martha discovered a refuge and shelter in the garden as well.

She can usually be found outside with a pack of enthusiastic dogs, capturing the magic of the garden with poems and a camera lens. *A Murmuration of Words* is her first poetry collection.